THE SONGS OF
ELTON JOHN

Wise Publications
London/New York/Sydney/Paris/Copenhagen/Madrid

CONTENTS

Exclusive Distributors:
Music Sales Limited
8/9 Frith Street,
London W1V 5TZ, England.
Music Sales Pty Limited
120 Rothschild Avenue
Rosebery, NSW 2018,
Australia.

Order No.AM950950
ISBN 0-7119-7066-1
This book © Copyright 1997 by Wise Publications
Visit the Internet Music Shop at
http://www.musicsales.co.uk

Unauthorised reproduction of any part of this publication by any
means including photocopying is an infringement of copyright.

Compiled by Peter Evans
Book design by Chloë Alexander

Printed in the United Kingdom by
Caligraving Limited, Thetford, Norfolk.

Your Guarantee of Quality
As publishers, we strive to produce every book to the highest
commercial standards. The book has been carefully designed to
minimise awkward page turns and to make playing from it a real
pleasure. Particular care has been given to specifying acid-free, neutral-
sized paper made from pulps which have not been elemental chlorine
bleached. This pulp is from farmed sustainable forests and was
produced with special regard for the environment. Throughout, the
printing and binding have been planned to ensure a sturdy, attractive
publication which should give years of enjoyment. If your copy fails to
meet our high standards, please inform us and we will gladly replace it.

Music Sales' complete catalogue describes thousands of titles and is
available in full colour sections by subject, direct from Music Sales
Limited. Please state your areas of interest and send a cheque/postal
order for £1.50 for postage to: Music Sales Limited, Newmarket Road,
Bury St. Edmunds, Suffolk IP33 3YB.

BENNIE AND THE JETS

WORDS & MUSIC BY ELTON JOHN & BERNIE TAUPIN

© Copyright 1973 for the world by Dick James Music Limited, 47 British Grove, London W4.
All Rights Reserved. International Copyright Secured.

(3rd time vocal) Say __ Can - dy and Ron - nie have you seen them yet __ but

they're __ so spaced out __ Ben - nie and the Jets

But __ they're weird and they're won-der-ful __ oh Ben - nie She's real - ly keen __ She's got e -

-lec-tric boots __ a mo-hair suit __ you know I read it in a mag - a - zine __ oh __

CANDLE IN THE WIND

WORDS & MUSIC BY ELTON JOHN & BERNIE TAUPIN

© Copyright 1973 for the world by Dick James Music Limited, 47 British Grove, London W4.
All Rights Reserved. International Copyright Secured.

Good-bye Nor - ma Jean _____ though I nev - er knew you at all _____
Good-bye Nor - me Jean _____ from the young man in the twen - ty sec - ond row_

_____ you had _____ the grace to hold your-self _____ while those a - round _____ you crawled_
_____ who sees you as some-thing more than sex - u - al _____ more than just Mar - i - lyn_ Mon-roe_

D.S. al Coda

And it

CODA

The can-dle had burned out

long _____ be - fore _____ your leg - end ev - er did. _____

DANIEL

WORDS & MUSIC BY ELTON JOHN & BERNIE TAUPIN

© Copyright 1972 for the World by Dick James Music Limited, 47 British Grove, London W4.
All Rights Reserved. International Copyright Secured.

GOODBYE YELLOW BRICK ROAD

WORDS & MUSIC BY ELTON JOHN & BERNIE TAUPIN

© Copyright 1973 for the world by Dick James Music Limited, 47 British Grove, London W4.
All Rights Reserved. International Copyright Secured.

DON'T LET THE SUN GO DOWN ON ME

WORDS & MUSIC BY ELTON JOHN & BERNIE TAUPIN

© Copyright 1974 for the World by Big Pig Music Limited/Warner Chappell Music Limited, 129 Park Street, London W1.
All Rights Reserved. International Copyright Secured.

I GUESS THAT'S WHY THEY CALL IT THE BLUES

WORDS & MUSIC BY ELTON JOHN, BERNIE TAUPIN & DAVEY JOHNSTONE

© Copyright 1983 for the World by Big Pig Music Limited/Warner Chappell Music Limited, 129 Park Street, London W1.
All Rights Reserved. International Copyright Secured.

ROCKET MAN

WORDS & MUSIC BY ELTON JOHN & BERNIE TAUPIN

© Copyright 1972 for the World by Dick James Music Limited, 47 British Grove, London W4.
All Rights Reserved. International Copyright Secured.

SACRIFICE

WORDS & MUSIC BY ELTON JOHN & BERNIE TAUPIN

© Copyright 1990 for the World by Big Pig Music Limited/Warner Chappell Music Limited, 129 Park Street, London W1.
All Rights Reserved. International Copyright Secured.

1. It's a hu - man sign When things go wrong

2. Mu - tual mis - un - der - stand- ing Af - ter the fact

When the scent of her ling - ers And temp - ta-tions strong

Sen - si - ti - vi - ty builds a pri-son In the fin - al act

into the boundary
We lose direction

of each married mind
No stone unturned

Sweet deceit comes a callin'
No tears to damn you

and negativity lands
When jealousy burns

cold cold heart

hard done by you

some things look better baby

just passing through

SOMEONE SAVED MY LIFE TONIGHT

WORDS & MUSIC BY ELTON JOHN & BERNIE TAUPIN

© Copyright 1975 for the World by Dick James Music Limited, 47 British Grove, London W4.
All Rights Reserved. International Copyright Secured.

1. When I think of those east end lights, mug-gy nights, the cur-tains drawn_ in the lit - tle room down stairs _____ Pri - ma-don - na, lord you real-ly should have been there. _ sit-ting like a prin-cess perched _ in her e - lec - tric chair. ____ And it's one more beer, _____ and I don't hear you

an-y-more.___ We've all ___ gone cra-zy late - ly, my friends out there___ roll - in' round___ the

base-ment floor. And some-one saved my life to-night,___ sug-ar bear.___

You al-most had your hooks in me,___ did-n't you, dear?___ You near - ly had me roped_ and tied,___

al - tar bound, ___ hyp- no-tised,_ sweet free-dom whis-pered in my ear. ___You're a but-ter-fly,___ and

Chorus 𝄋

but-ter-flies ___ are free ___ to fly, ___ Fly a-way ___ high-a-way ___ bye

bye.

To Coda
last time

And I would have walked head on ___ in-to the deep end of a riv-er, cling-ing to your stocks and bonds, ___ pay-ing your

Verse 2.   I never realized the passing hours
Of evening showers,
A slip noose hanging in my darkest dreams.
I'm strangled by your haunted social scene
Just a pawn out-played by a dominating queen.
It's four-o-clock in the morning
Damn it!
Listen to me good.
I'm sleeping with myself tonight
Saved in time, thank God my music's still alive.   **TO CHORUS**

YOUR SONG

WORDS & MUSIC BY ELTON JOHN AND BERNIE TAUPIN

© Copyright 1969 for the World by Dick James Music Limited, 47 British Grove, London W4.
All Rights Reserved. International Copyright Secured.

Slow, but with a beat

I'm don't _ have much | mon-ey, _____ but, | boy, if I did, _____
know _ it's not | much but it's _ the | best I can do, _____
But the sun's been quite | kind _____ | while I wrote this song, _____
An-y-way _ the | thing _____ is | what I real-ly mean, _____

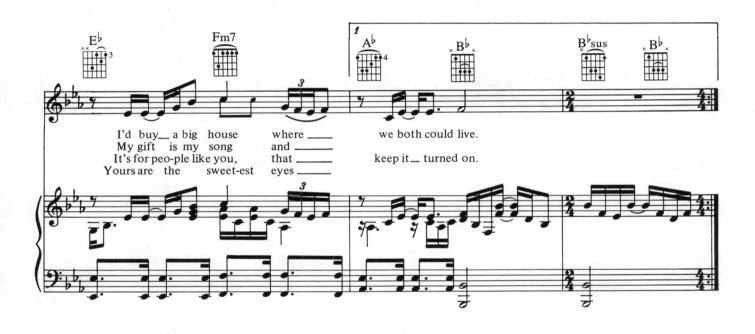

I'd buy _ a big house | where _____ | we both could live.
My gift is my song | and _____ |
It's for peo-ple like you, | that _____ | keep it _ turned on.
Yours are the sweet-est | eyes _____ |

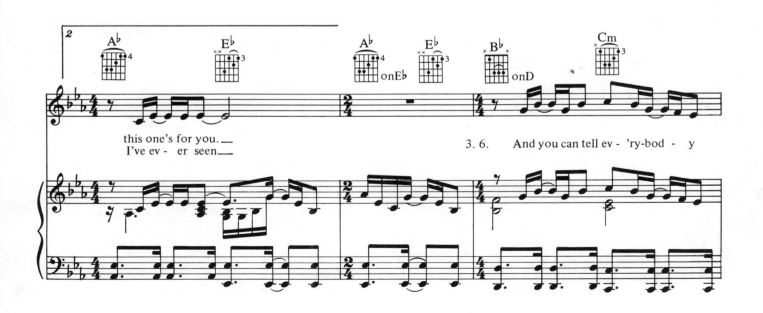

this one's for you. __
I've ev - er seen __

3. 6.   And you can tell ev - 'ry-bod - y

Fm7　　　Ab　　　Bb onD　　　Cm

This — is　your　song. _____　　It　may — be　quite — sim-ple but, —

Fm7　　　Ab　　　Cm　　　Cm onBb

Last time to Coda ⊕

now that it's done, _____　　I hope you don't mind, — I hope you don't mind —

Cm onA　　　Ab6　　　Eb onG　　　Ab6

_ that　I　put — down　in — words.　　How　won-der-ful　life　is — while

rit.

Ab　　　Bb　　　Bbsus　　　Bb

D.S. al Coda
with repeat

you're — in — the world. _____

a tempo

7.8. I hope you don't mind, __ I hope you don't mind __ that I put __ down in __ words, How

won - der - ful life is __ while you're __ in __ the world. __

you're __ in __ the world. __

SAD SONGS (SAY SO MUCH)

WORDS & MUSIC BY ELTON JOHN & BERNIE TAUPIN

© Copyright 1984 for the World by Big Pig Music Limited/Warner Chappell Music Limited, 129 Park Street, London W1.
All Rights Reserved. International Copyright Secured.

(So) Turn 'em on, _____ turn 'em on, _____ turn on those sad songs. _____ When all hope is gone _____ why don't you tune in and turn _____ them on? _____ They reach in - to your room, oh, _____ just feel _____ their _____ gen - tle touch. _____